A Complete Guide to
Pooled Income Funds
&
RETIREMENT INCOME THROUGH GIVING

A Complete Guide to
Pooled Income Funds
&
RETIREMENT INCOME THROUGH GIVING

Helping Clients Increase Retirement Income Using
Appreciated Assets & Turn-Key Charitable Trusts

By Mark D. Quam

MARKETPLACE BOOKS®
GLENELG, MARYLAND

TR

SEC

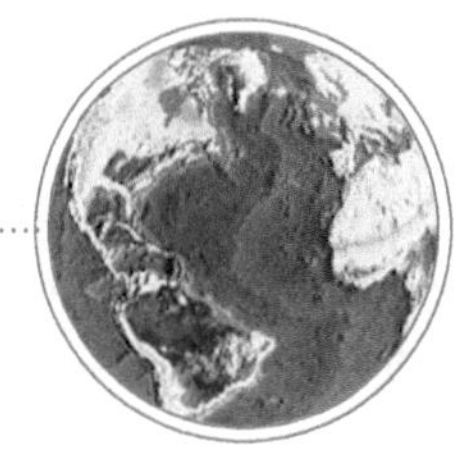

ISBN: 1-59280-353-9

ISBN 13: 978-1-59280-353-8

Printed in the United States of America.

Table of Contents

About the Author

Mark Quam is the Chief Executive Officer of Welton Street Investments LLC (WSI), located in Denver, Colorado. Quam is a member of FINRA Corporate Finance Committee.

WSI is also the Managing Broker/Dealer and distributor of the Life Income Funds of America. The Life Income Funds are a series of Pooled Income Funds that provide owners of appreciated real estate and securities with a turnkey charitable trust solution. The Life Income Funds are offered through a selling group of FINRA member firms.

www.LifeIncomeFund.org

Introduction

The purpose of this book is to give financial advisors a realistic solution that creates value, increases confidence, and attracts new business. This is the first in a series of Welton Street Investments retirement income planning solutions.

The current bear market/credit crisis/consumer retrenchment will be one for the ages and referenced for generations to come. I think it is important to mention this upfront because everyone has reason to pause, take a step back and try and see where things are headed. Things may never get back to what we used to call *normal.* This is the new normal. But here are the realities: Our clients will keep getting older; hunger for income will increase; taxes will move in a new direction and charitable giving will continue, if not increase. These realities create demand for Pooled Income Funds (PIFs).

Some estimate that there is $41 trillion of assets destined for generational transfer and $6 trillion of it will be left to nonprofits in a testamentary fashion. The confluence of current events has created incredible demand for monetizing real estate, creating lifetime income and using the $6 trillion earmarked in our last will and testament in the most tax-efficient manner. Unique times call for unique solutions. The following is an overview of Pooled Income Funds—how they work and how they can increase your clients' future income during our current difficult economic times.

Chapter 1

PIF Basics

Pooled Income Funds were introduced by the IRS as part of the 1969 Tax Reform Act. A PIF is a pre-built, turnkey equivalent to a Charitable Remainder Trust (CRT). By turnkey, I mean "off the shelf." Think of a PIF as an open-ended, mutual fund CRT that makes it easy and affordable to turn smaller positions of your clients' appreciated investments into lifetime income while providing a tax deduction and eliminating capital gains tax. PIFs are similar to mutual funds, ETFs, and other structured investments because they are continuously available to new donors. This means there are no set-up requirements, attorneys, or trustees to hire, and all of the ongoing administration and compliance is handled by the PIF's established trustees.

In my many years working with financial professionals, I have found that a majority of them have used some type of CRT with their clients. Yet most, if not all, have had negative experiences with CRTs. Pooled Income Funds offer a turnkey charitable trust solution, eliminating many, if not all of the problems advisors dislike about CRTs.

The Structure of the Pooled Income Fund

The traditional Pooled Income Fund is a deferred gift vehicle. As stated above, it is a pre-built, turnkey mutual fund equivalent to a charitable remainder trust (CRT). It is similar to mutual funds, ETFs, and other structured investments in the sense that Pooled Income Funds are continuously available to new donors.

A Pooled Income Fund is a trust that is established and maintained by a public charity, so as stated, there are no set-up requirements, lawyers, or trustees to hire, and all of the ongoing administration and compliance is handled by the established trustees.

The Pooled Income Fund receives contributions from donors that are commingled with other contributions for investment purposes. Once accepted, the donated funds are co-invested by the Pooled Income Fund into a diversified portfolio of income-focused investments based on the donor's risk tolerance and investment objectives. In the year of the donation, the donor may be entitled to a charitable contribution tax deduction, as well as other tax benefits.

Each donor is assigned "units of participation" in the fund, the issuance of which is based on a donor's contribution value relative to the overall value of the fund at the time of contribution. The fund's overall value is typically represented as the cumulative value of the outstanding units, and therefore the number of units issued is simply calculated by dividing the value of the contribution by the value of a unit.

Each unit represents the right to a pro rata share of the variable income of the Pooled Income Fund. The donor or a selected income beneficiary receives quarterly distributions of the pro rata share of the variable investment income generated by the fund.

Each year, the fund's entire net investment income is distributed to the income beneficiaries according to their units of participation. Distributions are made to each designated income beneficiary for his or her lifetime. There is no legal limitation to the number of beneficiaries a donor can designate, but most (not all) Pooled Income Funds restrict the income beneficiaries to two in order to reduce the overall administrative burden of the fund. Upon the death of the last income beneficiary, the portion of the fund assets attributable to the participant is severed from the fund and used by the charity for its charitable purposes. A Pooled Income Fund might therefore also be described as a charitable remainder mutual fund.

How a PIF Works

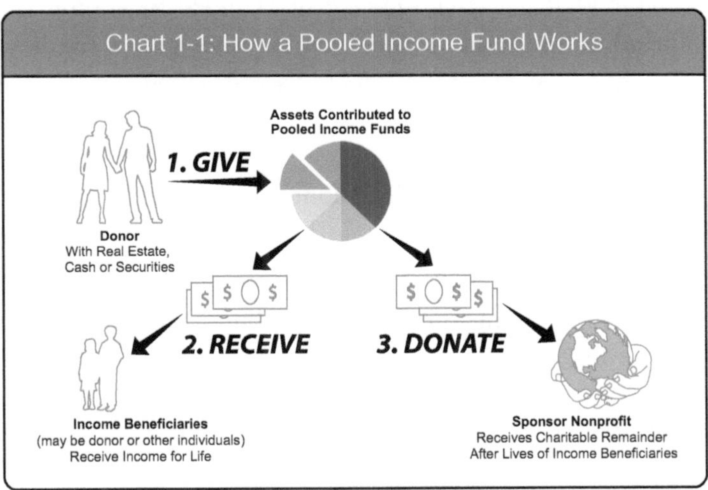

Your client becomes a donor to the Pooled Income Fund. The trust is already in place; all that needs to be executed is an Instrument of Transfer.

Although donors are well advised to have the (1) Disclosure Statement, (2) Declaration of Trust, and (3) Instrument of Transfer reviewed by their professional advisors, they will not incur the delay and expense of having an individual trust instrument created, as would be required with a charitable remainder trust.

The Four Benefits You Need to Know

A PIF:

• **Eliminates the capital gains tax on the property.** Contributions of long-term appreciated assets (real estate and liquid securities) may eliminate capital gains taxes. (Note: assets held for less than one year are not accepted.) Removing the asset from your estate may also reduce your heirs' tax liability.

• **Provides a tax deduction.** The donor realizes the tax advantages of charitable giving. Deductions are determined by several variables, including the value of the donation, the ages of the designated income beneficiaries, and the historical rate of return of the Pooled Income Fund to which the donor contributed.

• **Generates a lifetime income.** The donor may designate himself or herself as income beneficiary or, with some PIFs, multiple income beneficiaries may be named. For those planning their estates, this option allows the opportunity to provide life income for children and grandchildren.

• **Supports deserving nonprofits.** At the death of the last income beneficiary, the remaining principal is transferred to the establishing nonprofit.

Besides these four benefits, many PIFs allow donors to select from various pools that may include various professional money management funds and various income objectives.

Chapter 2

How to Jumpstart Your Clients' Retirement Income with PIFs

The number one concern[1] of the millions of people[2] about to retire: How can I increase retirement income from an already stretched-thin portfolio of assets? Before I answer this, I want to discuss the great opportunity that this question poses. Advisors who can answer the question of how to increase retirement income will not only gain their clients' confidence and retain their business, but they will also attract *new* business.

It is well known that consumers will pay premium prices for value. Clients will no doubt pay a premium price for the design and implementation of a truly unique method for solving their future income needs. Wall Street knows this, and, as I write this, their marketing machinery is working overtime, developing new angles on old products that will attempt to serve as the industry's

1 Dr. Ken Dychtwald, one of leading authorities on aging in America, explains it this way: "World War II had ended and men came home from four years of war without women. What happened? They start having babies; 10,000 babies a day, one every eight seconds, 4,000,000 a year for the next 18 years, and guess what, that same demographic has started turning 60 and they are about to retire; 10,000 people a day, one every eight seconds, 4,000,000 a year for the next 18 years."

2 *Financial Planning*, March 2008.

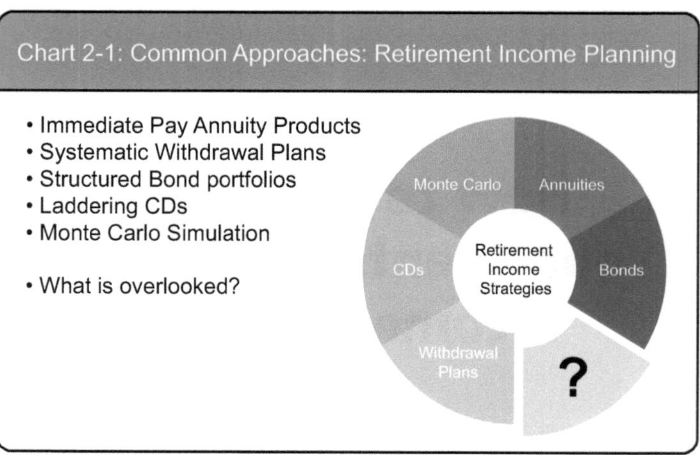

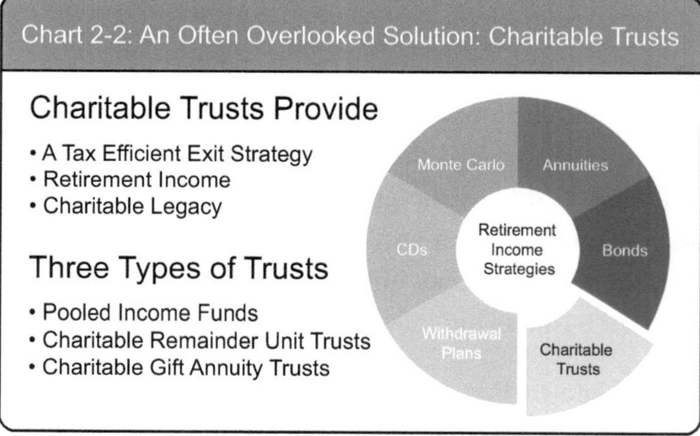

solution for increasing retirees' income. Unfortunately, no matter what marketing spin they come up with, the current batch of retirement income products is overly complex, not clear as to actual value, and most will be mere variations of traditional insurance and annuity products.

Imagine being able to speak with your clients about something positive and optimistic—the contribution to a deserving non-profit—during those difficult moments when they are trying to plan their retirement.

Today, the majority (8 out of 10) of US households donate to nonprofit organizations. More individuals donate to charity than vote, yet $25 billion of potential real estate donations is rejected annually.[3] Pooled Income Funds offer a way for those assets to be put to use, not only providing retirement income for the donor's chosen beneficiaries, but also fulfilling the growing demand for charitable giving. Bring this soution to your client and you will set your advice apart from tens of thousands of other financial professionals waiting for Wall Street to produce a new alternative.

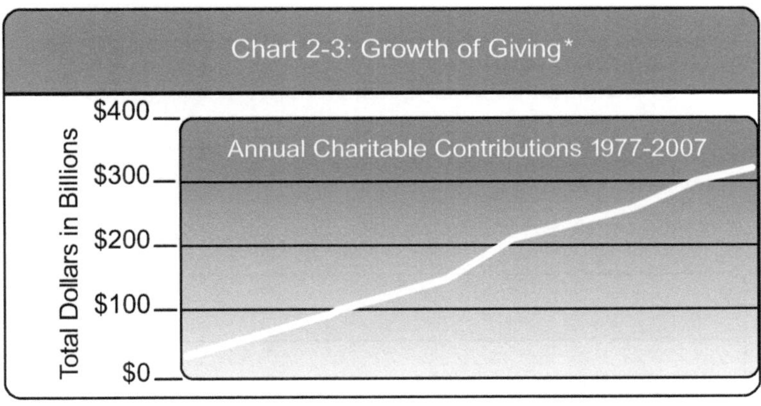

* Giving USA Foundation™ / Giving USA 2007

Most of us, including the financial advisors I have interviewed, do not expect Wall Street to come up with any viable solutions, especially now. This is where I see a tremendous opportunity for you, the financial advisor, to become proactive, not dependent on Wall Street for the next new income solution. You can build your own solutions with the potential to increase your clients' income using Pooled Income Funds that are already in the marketplace to monetize appreciated real estate and stock. You and your clients will see why the Pooled Income Fund strategy is especially transparent, understandable, and easily monitored.

3 Source: *Giving USA*, a publication of Giving USA Foundation™; researched and written by the Center on Philanthropy at Indiana University.

Chart 2-4: Charitable Giving Landscape

- **US Oil Imports in 2007** → $355 Billion *
- **Wal-Mart Revenue in 2007** → $379 Billion **
- **Charitable Giving in 2007** → $306 Billion ***

a.) Individuals	$229 Billion	75%
b.) Foundations	$ 38 Billion	13%
c.) Bequests	$ 23 Billion	7%
d.) Corporations	$ 15 Billion	5%

* US Total Crude Oil and Product Imports
U.S. Department of Energy – Energy Information Administration, July 28, 2008
Official Energy Statistics from the U.S. Government
<http://tonto.eia.doe.gov/dnav/pet/pet_move_impcus_a2_nus_ep00_im0_mbbl_a.htm>

** Wal-Mart: 2008 Annual Report

*** Giving USA FoundationTM /Giving USA 2007

Chart 2-5: Charitable Giving Market

- Overall Charitable Contributions
  - 89% of households give*
  - 2007 annual charitable contributions reached over $300 billion*
  - It is estimated that charitable contributions could exceed $55 trillion by 2052*
- Charitable Trusts (CRTs, CGAs, PIFs)
  - Over $125 billion in assets**
  - Largest charitable giving vehicle
  - PIFs are offered by all Ivy League Universities
  - Most Charitable trusts are created on a one-off basis by CPAs and attorneys
- Donor Advised Funds(DAF)
  - Over 37 financial institutions sponsored DAFs in 2007*
  - With over 107,000 account holders*
  - Approximately $21.7 billion assets*

* National Philanthropic Trust SM
2007 Philanthropy Statistics
<http://www.nptrust.org/philanthropy/philanthropy_stats.asp>

** Internal Revenue Service

Chapter 3

Educate Your Clients

Why should you start talking to your clients about a new income solution via Pooled Income Funds now? First, a lion's share of the population is no longer in wealth accumulation mode. 401(k)s are down 25-40%, depending on how they were invested. Other investments are down, old portfolio models no longer apply, and we've got to look somewhere else to meet clients' needs.

To initiate discussions on this opportunity with your clients, you could begin by sharing the following explanation to demonstrate why *now*, more than any other period in our lifetime, is the best time for clients to use appreciated assets to increase their retirement income.

Turn Real Estate into Income

Most families are sitting on a large part of their net worth in real estate—real estate that, on average, produces very little or no income. If somebody owns a non-institutional quality piece of real estate, like a rental home, a small apartment building, or, perhaps best, a piece of land that generates no income, that person is sitting on wealth but little or no distributable income. On average, over 50% of high net worth households own commercial property as an investment vehicle.[1] The baby boom demographic has created a huge demand for the sale of these highly appreciated assets to create cash flow through other sources, without the headaches associated with owning and managing property. Unfortunately, too often, the solution is to convert the asset into some version of a fixed investment vehicle. While this provides elements of immediate gratification, there are usually a number of substantial downsides—not the least of which is, before you can buy that annuity or CD, you have to sell your real estate and pay your taxes.

A Pooled Income Fund allows you to exit that real estate, eliminate taxes, and place your equity with professional money managers. Right now, everyone is looking for the best place to generate income, and this may be the best time in our financial history to invest with top-tier money managers.

Another benefit of the Pooled Income Fund concept is that the outside managers' investment objectives are generating income, not growth. They may have some fluctuation in the principal: a bond fund may go up, it may go down, but their primary objective is to create a steady income stream that you did not get when you owned a piece of farmland or a vacation home. Your clients are looking to replace the biggest bulk of their net worth—real estate—and you can provide the solution: a tax efficient, professionally managed lifetime income, combined with a charitable legacy.

---

1 Marcus & Millichap and Trusts & Estates, "Dangerously Detached: Wealth Advisors and Commercial Real Estate—A Special Research Report," October 2006.

PIF Benefits

- Tax-Efficient Solution
  - Charitable contribution tax deduction
  - Elimination of capital gains tax on contributed amount
  - Reduction of estate tax
- Lifetime Income
  - A lifetime of income distributions
  - Access to professionally managed funds
  - Ability to name multiple income beneficiaries
- A Charitable Legacy
  - Charity that establishes the PIF receives the charitable remainder interest
  - Some grant-making organizations that sponsor PIFs allow donors to recommend other deserving nonprofits to also receive their grants
- Modest Cost of Administration

Another significant advantage of the Pooled Income Fund is the relatively modest cost of administration—especially pertinent to today's conversations about real returns. Whereas charitable remainder trusts require the filing of tax and information returns for each individual trust, an organization maintaining a Pooled Income Fund is required to file only one set of returns regardless of the number of fund participants. Pooled Income Funds will provide the income beneficiaries with appropriate tax information for returns.

With this solution, you can now provide your clients with a vehicle (the Pooled Income Fund) that allows for the conversion of illiquid assets (highly appreciated real estate or company stock) into income-producing funds inside the Pooled Income Fund.

Chart 3-1: Often Overlooked Retirement Income Solutions

Reasons Trusts are Overlooked by Many Advisors

- Unfamiliar with solution set
- Familiar but frustrated with cost and complexity:
  - Legal expenses of formation
  - Legal compliance costs
  - Asset thresholds
  - Risk penalties
- Lack of compensation (CRTs and CGAs are used as asset retention strategies, not fee generators)
- Don't believe clients have a charitable intent

Pooled Income Funds provide the optimum solution strategy for persons who would like to dispose of highly appreciated, low-yielding property in favor of assets that will produce higher amounts of cash flow, especially since the client does not recognize a gain or loss on the transfer of property to a PIF [Reg. §1.642(c)-5(a)(3)].

It is important to also note the double tax leverage that can be accomplished by eliminating recognition of capital gain and creating an immediate charitable income tax deduction.

The Pooled Income Fund is not a new concept. Colleges and universities have used PIFs to attract money for decades. Charitable organizations regularly establish PIFs to which donors make contributions of cash or other property. However, approximately 80 percent of real estate donations to nonprofit organizations are declined.[2] But, the rediscovery of Pooled Income Funds may come just in time to provide a solution to the biggest challenge facing

2 Jennifer Forsyth, "Charities Begin at Home," *The Wall Street Journal*, August 16, 2006.

millions of retiring baby boomers. The balance of this book will explain the whys and hows in detail.

Chapter 4

How PIFs Work

Let's say your best client is about to retire and has a substantial portion (one million dollars) of his net worth in appreciated real estate. However, what is received in terms of income doesn't match the property's stated value. The client also has to deal with property taxes, mortgage costs, and the expenses associated with annual repair and maintenance and hands-on management. In the past, your client had only four choices:

1. **Do nothing.** Keep the property and all that is involved with managing real estate.

2. **Sell the property.** Reduce the asset by paying various capital gains and other taxes including recapture of depreciation. If you sold a million-dollar property, you could end up paying over $350,000 to the government in taxes, depending on what state you live in.

3. **Execute a 1031 Exchange.** You are simply deferring your tax bill, by having to buy another piece of real estate, and again, having to manage that property. A 1031 Exchange never works perfectly, and the odds of finding and closing on another million-dollar property within the regulatory timeframes is extremely difficult. Given some of the difficulties in complying with the strict 1031 Exchange

guidelines and the demand for management-free investments, experienced real estate companies have introduced two alternative investment products to the exchange market: (i) Tenant-in-Common investments (TIC) and (ii) Net Lease Properties.

4. **Donate it directly to a charity.** However, most charities do not accept real estate because of the liabilities associated with ownership. Yes, you can set up charitable remainder trusts, but those are expensive and involve estate-planning attorneys and CPAs.

The Fifth Alternative

Now, there is a fifth alternative that actually makes sense – contribute the property to a Pooled Income Fund.

Here is a simple example of how the Pooled Income Fund concept works.

Howard (age 67) and Mary (age 64) Peterson have been retired for four years. They own a highly appreciated piece of real estate (worth $750,000 with a tax basis of $100,000) and are in the 35% tax bracket. They are tired of managing their property and are deciding whether or not to sell it. The Petersons are looking for potentially better current income, diversification, elimination of management hassles and professional money management without having to pay an estimated $140,000 in capital gains taxes[1], in addition to any depreciation recapture taxes.

Sale price (fair market value) – tax basis (cost basis) = capital gain

Additionally, the federal tax on depreciation recapture is 25%. (Note: Our example shows no debt.)

---

1 15% maximum federal capital gains rate, plus an estimated 5% state capital gains rate, applied towards the potential recognized gain of $650,000. Check with your tax advisor to determine whether there are additional capital gains taxes due at the same state or local level.

- $750,000 fair market value
- $100,000 current tax basis
- $100,000 depreciation taken (so the original tax/cost basis was $200,000)
- Federal tax calculation would be:
  $750,000 – 200,000 = 550,000 cap gains @ 15% = $82,500
- $100,000 depreciation recap @ 25% = $25,000
- $750,000 – 100,000 = 650,000 state cap gain @ 5% = $32,500
- Total taxes owed = $140,000

By contributing their real estate to a Pooled Income Fund product that accepts real estate properties, the Petersons were able to eliminate capital gains and depreciation recapture taxes (to the extent that the property is a capital asset and not subject to a mortgage). Second, by having the entire $750,000 contributed, the Petersons receive income for life (assuming an estimated yield of 7%) of approximately $52,500 annually and approximately $1,312,500 during their lives (assuming joint life expectancy of 25 years after donation).

The Petersons understand that all income distributions are subject to federal and/or state tax.

Lastly, the Petersons are eligible to receive a current income tax deduction of $250,000 and, upon their death, the remainder principal is to be donated to the nonprofit organizations they recommended[2].

2 The calculation of the deduction will vary depending upon the PIF. The factor used to determine the deduction is based on income beneficiary(ies) life expectancy (using IRS actuarial tables) and the recent PIF disctribution rate.

Chapter 5

Not All PIFs are Alike

The ways in which Pooled Income Funds are alike, and their differences, cover an array of attributes: (i) number of income beneficiaries allowed; (ii) available investment alternatives; (iii) acceptable assets (some do not accept contributions of assets such as real estate or tradable securities); and (iv) ability to recommend the direction of the charitable remainder interest that, upon death of the last income beneficiary, reverts to the nonprofit that established the Pooled Income Fund.

While many Pooled Income Funds limit the number of income beneficiaries to two, under Section 642 (c)(5) of the Internal Revenue Code of 1986, as amended (the "Code"), a donor has the ability to name "one or more" living persons as the income beneficiaries.

Lastly, most Pooled Income Funds are established for the benefit of the nonprofit cause of the establishing organization. As such, the charitable remainder, upon death of the last income beneficiary, will revert to the sponsoring nonprofit organization and will be utilized solely in support of its nonprofit mission.

Some Pooled Income Funds have been established by grant-making organizations and, therefore, provide a donor with the ability to influence the grants by making recommendations of the nonprofit organizations he wishes to support. The board of directors of the nonprofit has the final say with regard to all grants. However, if the organizations recommended fit the criteria of the nonprofit's grant-making efforts, it is likely that the recommendations will be honored.

How Are the Assets Managed?

A written statement of investment objectives for each fund dictates how the assets are to be managed. Many organizations maintain several Pooled Income Funds, each one having different investment objectives. These objectives can include maximizing current distributable income, maximizing capital appreciation, or a combination of the two.

The majority of Pooled Income Funds are invested in a managed securities portfolio or mutual funds consisting of debt instruments for income, equities for income, and capital appreciation.

Choosing the right allocation to the pools is an important job, and not only because you are trying to provide your clients with income that fits their objectives and risk tolerance – the allocations you choose are final. The only way to adjust allocations in the future is to add funds to pools, since redemptions are not available when making irrevocable gifts.

Contributions to the Pooled Income Fund

All potential contributions of real estate or securities are subject to review and approval of each Pooled Income Funds trustee. In most cases, donors must have owned their real estate or securities for longer than one year, and the minimum acceptable contribution can be a low as $150,000 for real estate and $20,000 for securities. Some types of securities and real estate that may be acceptable include:

1) Stock with unknown, low, or zero basis
2) Publicly traded securities
3) Stock certificates
4) Restricted securities
5) Residential real estate
6) Rental property
7) Office buildings
8) Apartment buildings
9) Retail centers
10) Industrial properties
11) Vacation homes
12) Land

Stock with Unknown, Low, or Zero Basis

The Problem

Your clients have positions of stock with an unknown basis. And if you don't know the basis, the IRS assumes it is zero and imposes capital gains on every dollar received on the sale. Your clients don't want to sell them if it means such a big tax hit, and to make it worse, these stocks usually provide little or no dividend income. Typically, these stocks end up sitting in a brokerage account and are never sold. Your clients can't find a way to convert those assets into something everyone needs these days: retirement income.

The Dying Solution

Most advisors have a number of clients like this, who have held stock positions for years because they have no way of knowing the original basis. Others have clients who hold stock they earned as a company employee—with zero basis—and have the same problem. Their current strategy is to sit on the stock and pass it to the next generation, which could take advantage of the step-up in cost basis. But dying is not much of a strategy, or one that is best for their clients, especially those who can use more retirement income.

The Living Solution

Today, many advisors are using a vehicle created by the SEC in 1969 as a solution: the Pooled Income Fund (PIF). In the most basic terms, a PIF is an open-end charitable remainder trust. PIFs allow multiple individuals to donate appreciated assets (like unknown basis stocks) to a pre-established trust. First, the donor eliminates the capital gains and receives a tax deduction on the charitable contribution. Next, the proceeds are typically invested in income-oriented mutual funds, generating income to the client for the rest of his life. Clients may also choose to continue that life income for other family members after their own death. Finally, at the end of all income beneficiaries' lives, the principal may be granted to one or more charities as designated by the client.

Debt-encumbered Real Estate

If a donor transfers property to a Pooled Income Fund that is subject to indebtedness and the charity assumes the debt, the entire amount of the indebtedness is an amount realized by the donor for purposes of computing gain as a bargain sale under Internal Revenue Code §1011(b) and its regulations, since the charity is only receiving the net equity value of the contributed property and the donor is being relieved of the debt obligation (as such, not part of the contribution). In essence, the transaction is treated as though the charity has handed the donor cash in the amount of the indebtedness. The organization will weigh the potential investment risk and expense against the net benefit of the gift.

Accordingly, the donor will realize gains in an amount equal to that which would have been realized had the donor sold a fractional interest in the property in an amount equal to the indebtedness on the date of transfer.

The Code provides that a transfer of real or personal property by a disqualified person to a private foundation shall be treated as a prohibited sale or exchange if (a) the property is subject to a mortgage or similar lien which the private foundation assumes, or (b) it is subject to a mortgage or similar lien which a disqualified person placed on the property within the 10-year period ending on the date of transfer (to the trust). (IRC §4941(d)(2)(A))

Minimum Contributions

Some Pooled Income Funds accept contributions smaller than $20,000. By the very nature of their commingling requirements, Pooled Income Funds can more easily diversify investments, meet investment management account minimums, and adhere to a uniform investment policy. These features, combined with relatively simple tax reporting compliance, lend an economy of scale that permits charitable organizations to offer significantly lower minimums than those required for charitable remainder trusts.

Chapter 6

The Role of the Nonprofit

There are numerous nonprofits that use Pooled Income Funds to enhance their ability to generate ongoing contributions in support of their charitable causes and to expand its base of future financial capital for its programs. There is nothing within the Tax Reform Act of 1969 that limits a nonprofit to a single Pooled Income Fund. In fact, certain nonprofits have established multiple Pooled Income Funds, each with differing investment objectives.

Though most charities won't accept real estate because of the liabilities associated with ownership, ($25 billion a year is rejected[1]) a few universities and college endowments have sponsored some of the few Pooled Income Funds that accept real estate. In most of those instances, the real estate was property that could be used by the university or college, or was a local revenue-producing property for the school.

While a donor has the ability to identify his or her desired income beneficiaries for a specific contribution, the beneficiary of the

1 *Giving USA*, a publication of Giving USA Foundation TM; researched and written by the Center on Philanthropy at Indiana University.

charitable remainder interest is always the sponsoring nonprofit. Upon the death of the last income beneficiary, the corresponding unit value will be redeemed and the proceeds donated to the sponsoring nonprofit.

In addition to paying income to named individuals, the public charity—to or for the use of which the remainder interest is contributed—may also be designated as one of the beneficiaries of an income interest. The donor need not retain or create a life interest in all the income from the property transferred to the fund, provided any income not payable to an income beneficiary is contributed to the same public charity maintaining the fund. No charitable contribution deduction is allowed to the donor for the value of such income paid to the charity at the time of transfer or when payments are actually made [Reg. §1.642(c)-5(a)(2)]. Neither is such payment made to charity taxable to the noncharitable income beneficiary.

Chapter 7

Client / Advisor Benefits

Client (Donor) Benefits

There are numerous reasons for a donor to use a Pooled Income Fund as his or her planned giving vehicle. These reasons typically fall into three main categories: (i) tax benefits, (ii) lifetime income, and (iii) charitable legacy.

Tax Benefits

For donors contributing appreciated property such as securities, or real estate that they have held for more than one year, depending upon the specific facts and circumstances of an individual donation, the donor may receive:

- Charitable contribution income tax deduction;
- Elimination of capital gains tax; and
- Reduction of estate taxes for heirs.

Generally, no deduction is allowed for anything other than a donor's entire interest in property for income, gift, and estate tax deduction purposes unless the contribution takes the form of a charitable remainder annuity trust, charitable remainder unitrust, or Pooled Income Fund [IRC §§170(f) (A); 2522(c); and 2055(e)].

Lifetime Income

While each Pooled Income Fund has a different investment profile and, therefore, provides different levels of variable income, all Pooled Income Funds provide a distribution of the fund's income for the lives of the income beneficiaries. Some Pooled Income Funds provide access to professionally managed funds and provide a donor with the ability to diversify their investment sources of income through alternative investment objectives. The income distributions are available for a donor or to those whom a donor wishes to designate as the income beneficiaries. As such, the generation of lifetime income may be for longer than simply the life of the donor, as she has the ability to name other living individuals as the beneficiaries (son, daughter, grandson, granddaughter, etc.).

Charitable Legacy

Here again, the options vary depending upon the sponsoring nonprofit organization. For some Pooled Income Funds, the charitable remainder is used for the programs of the sponsoring nonprofit organization to support its specific cause. For those nonprofit sponsors that are grant-making organizations, a donor may have the ability to recommend a broader use of her ultimate donation upon death of the last income beneficiary. In the latter instance, a donor has the ability to more broadly direct the creation of his ultimate charitable legacy and support multiple deserving nonprofit organizations.

Financial Advisor Benefits

- Additional appeal to your current clients:
  - Retirement income solution
  - Charitable trust solution
  - Appreciated assets solution

- Retain assets:
  - Retain assets that might otherwise be liquidated due to tax and estate-planning decisions
- Activate assets:
  - Turn dormant assets such as appreciated stock and real estate into managed assets
- Multi-generational philanthropic tool:
  - Build a long-term relationship with clients and their families

The benefit to the financial advisor is multi-layered but most importantly, this tool provides leadership and generates client confidence.

The solicitation of donations for a Pooled Income Fund is considered the offering of a security, and, therefore, if offered by someone outside the charity for compensation, must be offered by FINRA member firms and their respective registered representatives.

Financial Advisor Compensation

Typical compensation ranges between 0 and 5.5 percent upfront sales commission and 25 to 100 basis point annual servicing fees. Pooled Income Funds fall under the Philanthropy Protection Act of 1995, providing exemption from registration under the Securities Act of 1933, the Securities Exchange Act of 1934, as well as from the Investment Company Act of 1940, as amended.

While Pooled Income Funds are exempt from SEC registration, their marketing requires certain disclosure and financial reporting, and there are restrictions on transfers of interests and on contributions. Pooled Income Funds are also subject to the antifraud provisions of federal securities laws (and in some cases may be subject to certain state law requirements). There are no limitations on general solicitation or advertising, or any requirement that donors must satisfy the accredited investor limitations imposed by the private offering exemption in the Securities Act Section 4(2) and SEC Regulation D.

Summary: The Golden Age of Philanthropy

Chart S-1: The Future of Giving[1]
A.) Wealth Transfer Over the Next 20 Years...............$12 Trillion
B.) Charitable Bequests* Over the Next 20 Years........$1.7 Trillion
C.) Wealth Transfers Over the Next 55 Years.............$41 Trillion
D.) Charitable Bequests* Over the Next 55 Years........$ 6 Trillion
*Bequests are assets given to non-profits via will.

[1] National Philanthropic Trust SM
2007 Philanthropy Statistics
<http://www.nptrust.org/philanthropy/philanthropy_stats.asp>

If these studies are correct, the baby boomers will earmark $6 trillion of gifts in their wills. The use of planned gifts like PIFs can turn the $6 trillion into much needed retirement income for boomers today.

With baby boomers owning 57% of all vacation homes and 58% of all rental properties, many U.S. families have large amounts of their net worth locked-up in real estate equity. To realize this appreciation, the property must be sold. When selling real estate, many owners are faced with potentially large capital gains taxes, depreciation recapture, and the need to meet their fast approaching retirement plans. Thus, many owners share these common goals:

1. Exiting highly appreciated real estate

2. Eliminating capital gains tax

3. Eliminating property management obligations

4. Creating or continuing to receive income

5. Owning higher quality investments

6. Increasing diversification

7. Lowering estate taxes

By constructing your own programs that focus on increasing your clients' income, you will be meeting one of the greatest challenges facing the retired and the retiring. As a financial manager providing solutions and new ideas, you are also providing leadership and confidence just when American investors need it most. In addition, this strategy incorporates full transparency by using traditional investments and tax saving procedures that are easily understood by most investors. Finally, the benefits of Pooled Income Fund strategies only increase over time as the power of compounding rate increases becomes more evident. Your clients' Pooled Income Fund portfolio has the potential added benefit of providing an income stream that outpaces the increasing cost of living while providing tax efficiencies.

This single alternative meets all of these goals and offers a scalable and effective exit strategy for clients owning appreciated assets, such as real estate. By offering a Pooled Income Fund strategy, you will be adding value to your clients' portfolios and further strengthening your relationship with them. Both you and your clients will rest easy knowing that this is a strategy that has worked time and time again — one that is not just a fad or the creation of Wall Street marketing departments.

10 Top Pooled Income Funds

The following are some of the pooled income offerings available today. Please check each carefully to assure the attributes you are looking for in a planned giving vehicle are available:

1. Life Income Funds of America: www.lifeincomefund.org
2. Fidelity Charitable Gift Fund: www.charitablegift.org
3. Harvard University: www.haa.harvard.edu
4. Yale University: www.yale.planyourlegacy.org
5. Princeton University: www.princeton.org
6. Columbia University: www.columbia.planyourlegacy.org
7. Raymond James Charitable Endowment Fund: www.myfamilyfoundation.org
8. American Red Cross: www.redcross.org
9. Silicon Valley Community Foundations: www.siliconvalleycf.org
10. New York Presbyterian Hospital: www.nyp.org

Pooled Income Funds That Accept Real Estate

The following are some of the pooled income funds that accept real estate.

1. Life Income Funds of America: www.lifeincomefund.org
2. Harvard University: www.haa.harvard.edu
3. Columbia University: www.columbia.planyourlegacy.org

Appendix A: Advisor Quick Start Guide

Instead of waiting for Wall Street to solve the income problem, take the following actions described by these two selling strategies.

Stock with Unknown, Low, or Zero Basis

STEP ONE – List of clients who can use more income.

The exercise begins by combing through your book to uncover any long-term holdings with perhaps low or unknown cost basis. Don't overlook company stock received as compensation. Make a list of these clients and determine who would welcome more retirement income. This is your call list.

STEP TWO – The easiest call you have made in years.

"The other day we were talking about retirement income and I have some good ideas. You known the XYZ stock you have held for 20 years? We never talk about it because we don't know the basis and don't want to pay capital gains tax. Would you be interested in turning that into retirement income, eliminating the capital gain and receiving a tax deduction?"

What do you think the answer will be?

STEP THREE – Set up an appointment to discuss Pooled Income Funds.

Your clients will welcome the prospect of turning stagnant stocks into retirement income, tax benefits and the beginning of their charitable legacy.

Appreciated Real Estate

STEP ONE – Look past the obvious.

Most investors mistakenly overlook their appreciated real estate for additional sources of income because they think that they can't afford to sell it. Ask your clients if they own vacation homes, rental properties, commercial buildings or land. My bet is you will be surprised by more than one client who owns real estate that you did not know about.

STEP TWO – Go through your book of clients with appreciated investments ($20,000 minimum). Determine which of those clients could use a tax deduction and more income. Remember to ask clients about investments they have at other firms, as the other firm may not have access to the Pooled Income Funds.

STEP THREE – Make a call to introduce a new retirement income solution.

This is a solution your competitors are not calling about. Tell your clients you have good news.

1) They have appreciated assets.
2) You have a way to realize the appreciation without capital gains tax.
3) They may receive a tax deduction upon monetizing the assets.

4) You can provide income for their lives and lives of their heirs.
5) They will be building their charitable legacy.

Can we schedule a time to discuss this strategy face to face?

Appendix B: Pooled Income Fund Qualification

Pooled Income Fund Definition

The 1969 Tax Reform Act provides the authority for certain qualified charitable organizations to establish Pooled Income Funds. A Pooled Income Fund is created to receive, hold, manage, and reinvest property transferred to the fund by at least two individual donors. The general requirements for a Pooled Income Fund are outlined within Code Section 642(c)(5), which defines a Pooled Income Fund as an irrevocable trust established and maintained by a public charity, to which many donors can make contributions and receive income distributions. Section 642(c)(5) states that a Pooled Income Fund is a trust:

(a) to which each donor transfers property, contributing an irrevocable remainder interest in such property to or for the use of an organization described in section 170(b)(1)(A) (other than in clauses (vii) or (viii)), and retaining an income interest for the life of one or more beneficiaries (living at the time of such transfer),

(b) in which the property transferred by each donor is commingled with property transferred by other donors who have made or make similar transfers,

(c) which cannot have investments in securities that are exempt from taxes imposed by this subtitle,

(d) which includes only amounts received from transfers that meet the requirements of this paragraph,

(e) which is maintained by the organization to which the remainder interest is contributed and of which no donor or beneficiary of an income interest is a trustee, and

(f) from which each beneficiary of an income interest receives income, for each year for which he is entitled to receive the income interest referred to in subparagraph (A), determined by the rate of return earned by the trust for such year.

For purposes of determining the amount of any charitable contribution allowable by reason of a transfer of property to a pooled fund, the value of the income interest shall be determined on the basis of the highest rate of return earned by the fund for any of the three taxable years immediately preceding the taxable year of the fund in which the transfer is made. In the case of funds in existence less than three taxable years preceding the taxable year of the fund in which a transfer is made, the rate of return shall be deemed to be 6% per annum, except that the Secretary may prescribe a different rate of return.

Qualified Organizations

Nonprofit organizations that may establish, operate and are qualified to be the holder of the remainder interest for a Pooled Income Fund are described under Section 170(b)(1)(A) of the Code. Qualified organizations include the following:

(a) churches or conventions or associations of churches;

(b) educational organizations with regular faculty and curriculum and a regular student body attending resident classes;

(c) hospitals;

(d) organizations directly engaged in continuous research in conjunction with hospitals;

(e) organizations operated exclusively to hold and administer property for state and municipal colleges and universities and governmental units; and

(f) publicly supported organizations.

Specifically excluded under Code Section 642(c)(5)(A), however, are private operating foundations and supporting organizations as described in IRC 509(a)(2) and (3) unless they fit into one of the categories of public charities mentioned above (even though these organizations are also considered public charities for income tax deduction purposes). Private non-operating foundations are also excluded.

A Pooled Income Fund may not benefit more than one charitable remainder. In other words, there can be only one holder of the charitable remainder for contributions to a Pooled Income Fund. In the event the charitable organization maintaining a Pooled Income Fund goes out of existence or otherwise loses its qualification as a public charity, the trustees are required to select an alternate qualifying organization within 60 days after the organization ceases to exist or within 60 days of the expiration of the period in which a pleading can be filed to contest the loss of qualification [Rev. Rul. 85-57, 1985-1 C.B].

The Governing Instrument

While a Pooled Income Fund is not required to qualify as a trust under local law, it is taxed as a split interest trust and must file a Split-Interest Trust Information Return (Form 5227) for federal tax purposes. The governing instrument of a Pooled Income Fund is the declaration of trust. IRS Revenue Procedure 1988-53 contains a model Pooled Income Fund trust document. Any substantial modifications to this model trust document should be presented to the Internal Revenue Service for review.

In order to qualify as a Pooled Income Fund, the trust must meet all of the requirements set forth in the Code, the regulations promulgated thereunder, Revenue Rulings, and Procedures. (See: Rev. Rul. 72-196, 1972-1 C.B. 194; superseded, clarified, and amplified by Rev. Rul. 82-38, 1982-1 C.B. 96; amplified by Rev. Rul. 85-57, 1985-1 C.B. 182 ; and Rev. Rul. 90-103, 1990-2 C.B. 159 .) In Rev. Proc. 97-3, the IRS announced that it will continue its policy of not issuing advance rulings regarding whether a transfer to a Pooled Income Fund described in section 642(c) of the Code qualifies for charitable income, gift, or estate tax deductions under sections 170(f)(2)(A), 2522(c)(2)(A) or 2055(e)(2)(A), Rev. Proc. 97-3, 1997-1 I.R.B. 84. The IRS will, however, continue to rule regarding provisions that deviate from those found in the sample documents published in the Revenue Procedures.

Commingling Requirement

The declaration of trust as the governing instrument of a Pooled Income Fund requires that all property transferred to a Pooled Income Fund by each donor must be commingled with all property transferred to the fund by other donors. The other donations must meet the same requirements outlined above. The fund may be invested jointly with property held by or for the use of the sponsoring charitable organization, provided that the income of the Pooled Income Fund's investments is easily identifiable. Charitable organizations are permitted to operate multiple Pooled Income Funds, provided that each such fund is maintained by the nonprofit sponsor organization. Many of the large universities and certain other Pooled Income Fund sponsors maintain more than a single Pooled Income Fund in order to offer potential donors alternative investment strategies.

All contributed property must only be transferred under arrangements that meet the rules as outlined under Section 642(c)(5) and the terms of the declaration of trust.

Prohibited Investment Assets

Tax-Exempt Securities

The property transferred to the fund by any donor must not include any securities, the income from which is exempt from tax under subtitle A of the Code, and the fund must not invest in such securities. The governing instrument of the fund must contain specific prohibitions against accepting or investing in such securities [Reg. §1.642(c)-5(b)(4)]. In addition, if a Pooled Income Fund's assets are jointly invested in a common trust fund or with other assets of the sponsoring charitable organization, the investments held thereunder may not include tax-exempt securities as so defined.

Depletable or Depreciable Property

The IRS required in the Revenue Ruling 1990-103 that the governing declaration of trust for a Pooled Income Fund which does not expressly prohibit a trustee from accepting depreciable or depletable assets must require a creation of a depreciation reserve pursuant to generally accepted accounting principles. Failure to include the necessary provisions may disqualify a Pooled Income Fund.

Charitable Remainder

When a donor contributes property to a Pooled Income Fund, the contribution must be irrevocable. The irrevocable interest in the remainder of the contributed property is transferred for the use of the sponsoring public charity (the sole designated holder of the charitable remainder interest in the Pooled Income Fund). Upon contribution, a donor will either retain an income interest or designate an income interest for one or more living individuals upon the date of the contribution. The income interests created upon the contribution are typically represented by the issuance of units in the Pooled Income Fund and are lifetime income interests. Upon the death of the last remaining income beneficiary, the trustee shall sever the value of the remainder interest of the contribution from the fund and pay such amount to the sponsoring charitable organization.

The charitable remainder may not benefit more than one sponsoring nonprofit organization. In other words, there can be only one sponsoring organization that is the designated recipient of the charitable remainder interest of the fund. The income interests retained or designated by the donor are lifetime income interests and could be at risk if the sponsoring nonprofit organization ceases to exist. The IRS provided, in Revenue Ruling 1985-57, the trustee the authority to select a replacement charitable holder of the remainder interest if the sponsoring charitable organization ceases to exist or qualify at the time of termination of an income interest. Additionally, within the model declaration of trust outlined in Revenue Ruling 1988-53, the IRS provided the following sample language:

> If at the time of severance of the remainder interest Public Charity has ceased to exist or is not a public charity (an organization described in clauses (i) through (iv) of section 170(b)(1)(A) of the Code), the amount severed shall be paid to an organization selected by the Trustee that is a public charity.

Fund Maintenance Requirements

In order to meet the maintenance requirements outlined within Code Section 642(c)(5), the sponsoring charitable organization must exercise control over the Pooled Income Fund. The requirement is satisfied where the public charity exercises control directly or indirectly over the fund. For example, this requirement of control shall ordinarily be met when the public charity has the power to remove the trustee or trustees of the fund and designate a new trustee or trustees.

It is typical to see a bank act as the trustee for a Pooled Income Fund created by a qualified charity; however, the public charity retains the right to remove and replace such an institution with a new trustee.

Trustee Requirements

The governing instrument of the fund must prohibit a donor or income beneficiary of a Pooled Income Fund from serving as a trustee of the fund, and include a prohibition against self-dealing. No donor or beneficiary shall have any direct or indirect general responsibilities with respect to the Pooled Income Fund that are ordinarily exercised by the trustee [Reg. §1.642(c)-5(b)(6); Reg. §1.642(c)-5(a)(6)].

Under the regulations outlined within the federal tax code, the sponsoring charitable organization may designate itself as the trustee. However, certain state laws may restrict organizations' ability to make such a designation. Most funds are maintained by institutional trustees, but as noted previously, the sponsoring organization must maintain the power to remove or replace such institutions.

The prohibition against donors or beneficiaries serving as trustees extends to members of the sponsoring nonprofit's board of directors. A member of the board of directors may not be a donor or beneficiary of the Pooled Income Fund. The governing declaration of trust must prohibit board members, officers, and other officials who directly or indirectly participate in the fund management or oversight from being donors to or beneficiaries of the Pooled Income Fund.

To the extent the board of directors of the sponsor organization has hired an institution, such as a bank, to act as trustee for the Pooled Income Fund, such institutions typically charge fees for their services. The payment of administrative expenses associated therewith may be paid from the charitable holder of the remainder interest without jeopardizing the fund's qualification and will not constitute self-dealing that is prohibited under Code Section 4941.

Income Requirements

The governing declaration of trust must require the distribution of all net income from the Pooled Income Fund to the designated income beneficiaries during the taxable year in which the income is earned. If necessary, Section 642(c) provides that the trustee may make adjustment payments following the close of the fund's taxable year in order to insure the beneficiaries have received all of the fund's net income for that year. Such adjusting payments must be made on or before the sixty-fifth day following the close of the Pooled Income Fund's taxable year.

For purposes of income distributions to the beneficiaries, net income is generally defined as receipts that are classified as income in accordance with fiduciary accounting principles, less expenses. The amount of income distributable to the beneficiaries is dependent upon the rate of return for the fund for the given taxable year. All income must be distributed proportionally based upon the value of a donor's contribution to the Pooled Income Fund relative to the total value contributed assets as of the date of the contribution. The governing declaration of trust may provide for issuance of units representing proportional participation in the income of the fund.

In order to determine the respective proportional interest and, therefore, the number of units issued upon contribution of property, all units are of equal value and each represents a proportionate undivided interest in the fund. The trustee shall revalue each unit on a regular basis (at a minimum annually) by dividing the net valuation of the entire Pooled Income Fund by the number of outstanding units as of the valuation date. The number of units issued as of a contribution would then be determined by dividing the fair market value of the contributed property by the value of a unit in the fund immediately prior to the contribution.

Tax Reporting for the Funds

Pooled Income Funds are required to file, by April 15, the following tax forms on an annual basis:

- Form 1041: *U.S. Income Tax Return for Estates and Trusts*
- Form 5227: *Split-Interest Trust Information Return*

To the extent there is net income that is not required to be distributed, currently there would need to be a Form 1041-A filed (*Trust Accumulation of Charitable Amounts*). Additionally, if certain excise tax liabilities exist, the fund must also file a Form 4720: *Return of Certain Excise Taxes on Charities.* In addition, the trustee is responsible for assuring that each of the income beneficiaries receives a 1041 Form K-1.

Appendix C: Tax Implications for Donors and Beneficiaries

Income Tax Charitable Deduction

Deduction Calculation

A donor who makes an irrevocable gift to a Pooled Income Fund is entitled to a federal income tax charitable deduction for the year in which the gift is made. The amount of a donor's deduction is equal to the present value of the remainder interest of the donor's contribution as calculated under the Treasury Regulation §1.642(c)-6. The valuation of the remainder interest depends on the fair market value of the contribution, the age of the named income beneficiaries and the rate of return of the Pooled Income Fund. Actuarial tables published by the IRS are used to determine a factor for the value of the charitable remainder interest. This factor is multiplied by the value of the contribution in order to determine the amount of the charitable income tax deduction. The longer income is expected to be paid to an income beneficiary, the lower the charitable contribution deduction.

The rate of return used in the tax deduction calculation is equal to the highest annualized rate of return for any one of the three years immediately preceding the year of the contribution. If the Pooled Income Fund does not have three years of history, the rate of return to be used in the discounted value determination is the interest rate that is one percent less than the highest annual average of the monthly Code Section 7520 rates for the three calendar years immediately preceding the calendar year in which the transfer to the fund is made. Typically, the trustee provides information to assist the donor and the donor's tax advisor with the income tax deduction for each contribution.

Under federal income tax law, certain limitations apply to the amount of the charitable deduction a taxpayer may claim in any given year. In general, the deduction for an individual donor's aggregate charitable contributions of cash (or of non-appreciated property) within a single tax year is limited to 50 percent of the donor's adjusted gross income (computed without regard to the charitable deduction and any net operating loss carry-back). If an individual donor's charitable contributions exceed the applicable limitations, any excess contributions can be carried forward and deducted over the following five years. Additional limitations are placed on contributions of capital gain property, which should include most contributions of real estate or appreciated securities. For such contributions, the charitable contribution deduction is generally limited to 30 percent of the donor's adjusted gross income, unless the donor elects to claim the donor's basis in the contributed property (rather than the property's fair market value) as the amount of the charitable contribution. Where the taxpayer has so elected, the 50 percent limitation applies.

Claiming a Deduction

In order for a donor to be entitled to claim a charitable contribution with respect to contributions in excess of $500, the donor must receive written substantiation of the contribution from the Pooled Income Fund. The written substantiation must include the amount of the contribution and a description thereof, an indication as to whether the charity provided any goods or services to the donor, and a good faith estimate of the value of any goods and services provided to the donor. The acknowledgement must be in the hands of the donor prior to the earlier of 1) the date on which the donor files a return for the taxable year in which the contribution was made, or 2) the due date (including extensions) for filing such return.

For assets without a readily available fair market value, such as real estate, there is an additional requirement for the federal income tax laws that the donor will need to satisfy in order to claim a charitable contribution deduction. That is, the donor must obtain an appraisal supporting the valuation of the real estate and file a Form 8283 with their tax return. The Form 8283 must include a signature from an appraiser and the charity which contains the fair market value of the contribution.

Capital Gains

A donor realizes no taxable capital gains (or losses) as a result of making a contribution to a Pooled Income Fund, provided that the contributed property is not subject to any indebtedness.

This provides the donor with an opportunity to contribute low basis but highly appreciated assets such as securities or real estate without owing capital gains on the fair market value of the appreciated property. If such assets were sold prior to contribution to a Pooled Income Fund, the donor would owe taxes on the capital gains realized. However, if such assets are contributed to a Pooled Income Fund, the donor will receive the benefits of a charitable tax deduction and income without having to pay taxes on the capital gains.

A Pooled Income Fund pays no capital gains taxes on the sale of appreciated assets that had been held for more than a year prior to being contributed. The fund takes over the donor's holding period and basis. If the contributed property had been held for less than one year and then was sold by the Pooled Income Fund, the fund may owe taxes on the capital gains. For this reason, most Pooled Income Funds will not accept contributions of properties held for less than one year.

Gift and Estate Tax Considerations

Gifts made to charity via a Pooled Income Fund qualify for unlimited gift and estate tax deductions for the present value of the remainder interest. However, a gift or estate tax can be generated on the value of the retained income interest if it is transferred to someone other than the donor, the donor's spouse, or charity.

Gift Tax

If the donor is the sole income beneficiary of the contribution to a Pooled Income Fund, the contribution will not result in any gift tax. If the donor names one or more income beneficiaries, other than the donor, to receive income from the contribution, the contribution may be considered a gift, and therefore subject to gift tax. However, the contribution may be eligible for the annual gift tax exclusion of $12,000 per beneficiary or $24,000 per beneficiary if the donor's spouse agrees to join in the gift (these amounts are indexed for inflation). Additionally, if the donor is the first of two consecutive beneficiaries and reserves the right to revoke the beneficial income interest of a second beneficiary, there will be no taxable gift at the time of the contribution. The retention of a right to revoke prevents the donor from making a completed, and therefore taxable, gift. The retention of the right will result in the value of the secondary income interest in the donor's estate and should only be used where the donor is the first income beneficiary.

In addition, if the donor's spouse is an initial income beneficiary and is a citizen of the United States, the donor may elect on his or her tax return to treat the spouse's interest as a qualified terminable interest and thus qualify the interest for the unlimited gift tax marital deduction. If the donor's spouse is not a citizen of the United States, the value of his or her income interest may qualify for the annual exclusion for gifts to non-citizen spouses. Finally, even if the contribution to the fund should result in a potentially taxable gift, the donor may not have to pay any current tax, since under present federal law each person is entitled to make lifetime transfers of up to $1 million free from gift tax. However, any credit the donor uses against gift tax in one year reduces the amount of credit he or she is able to use against gift tax in subsequent years.

Taxable Gift with Donor and Non-Donor Income Recipients

If the donor and a non-donor are co-income recipients, the amount of the taxable gift depends on whether the non-donor has a concurrent or successive income interest.

Non-Donor as Primary Life Income Recipient and Donor as Successor

When a non-donor is the primary income recipient for life followed by the donor, the amount of the taxable gift is equal to the present value of the income interest based on the non-donor's life. In other words, the presence of the donor as a successor income recipient has no impact on the non-donor's receipt of the income interest. The computation of the taxable gift is therefore no different than if the non-donor is the sole income recipient of the trust.

Donor as Primary Life Income Recipient and Non-Donor as Successor

When the donor is the primary income recipient followed by the non-donor as successor income recipient, the taxable gift is equal to the present value of the non-donor's survivor income interest. It is equal to the difference between the present value of the income interest based on the donor's and non-donor's joint lives and the present value of the income interest based solely on the life of the primary income recipient (donor). An example is the case of a father naming himself as the primary income recipient and his son as the successor.

Donor and Non-Donor Joint and Survivor Life Income Recipients

When the income amount is payable to the donor and non-donor in equal shares for each of their lives with the decedent's portion payable to the survivor, the donor has, in essence, made two gifts: (a) the present value of the non-donor's right to receive a survivor income interest from one-half of the transfer, and (b) the present value of income interest for the income recipients' joint lives from the remaining one-half of the transfer.

Estate Tax Consequences when Right of Revocation is Absent

If the donor does not reserve the right to revoke her beneficiary children's interests, the gifts become complete at the time the transfer is made to the fund. Furthermore, the value of the trust will not be includible in her estate. In such a case, the donor will file a gift tax return for the value of the income interest that exceeds the $10,000 annual exclusion per recipient. The donor's unified gift tax credit is applied to the balance of any gift tax due. When the donor dies, the value of the original taxable gift is included in the calculation of her estate tax, with any prior gift taxes paid or unified credit used, credited against her tentative estate tax liability.

Estate Tax Consequences

If the donor is either the sole income beneficiary or the first of consecutive beneficiaries of the contribution to the Life Income Funds, the entire value of the units attributable to the contribution, generally computed as of the date of the donor's death, will be included in his estate for federal estate tax purposes. If there is no successor non-charitable income beneficiary, the donor's estate will be able to claim an offsetting charitable deduction equal to the entire amount included in the estate.

If the donor has named a successor to receive the income from the contribution, and after the donor's death, that successor has not had her right to receive income revoked through a will, the donor's estate may claim a charitable deduction for federal estate tax purposes only for the value of the charitable remainder interest. As a result, the value of the successor beneficiary's future income interest (based on the successor beneficiary's age at the time of the donor's death) may be included in the donor's estate for federal estate tax purposes.

If the donor's spouse is the successor beneficiary and she is a United States citizen, the legal representative of the donor's estate may elect to qualify the income interest for the unlimited federal estate tax marital deduction, thereby eliminating federal estate tax liability. If the successor beneficiary is not the donor's spouse or if the donor's spouse is not a United States citizen, no deduction will be available for the value of that income interest. The applicable exclusion amount that the donor's estate is entitled to use may be available to eliminate or reduce this possible estate tax liability. Under current federal law, each person is entitled to make transfers of up to $2 million at death, free from federal estate tax. However, that amount is reduced to the extent the federal gift tax exemption is used during life.

Marital Deduction

The rules concerning the qualification of transfers to Pooled Income Funds for marital gift and estate tax deduction purposes are complex and, if not properly planned, may unintentionally generate a transfer tax.

A transfer to a Pooled Income Fund that names a spouse as an income recipient is considered a gift of a terminable interest; however, unlike transfers to charitable remainder trusts, the transfer will not qualify for the gift tax marital deduction. Donors should, therefore, avoid making a completed gift at the time of transfer by reserving the right, exercisable by will, to revoke the spouse's income interest. Annual gifts will accrue to the spouse as income is received and will qualify for the gift tax marital deduction.

In the event the donor predeceases the spouse, the fair market value of the fund units will be includible in the donor spouse's estate under IRC §2044.

The donor's estate can, provided the surviving spouse is the sole income beneficiary, make an election to treat the present value of the remaining income interest as qualified terminable interest property (QTIP) thereby qualifying for the estate tax marital deduction. The present value of the remainder interest balance will qualify for the estate tax charitable deduction under IRC §2055. The estate tax marital deduction will not be available, however, if the couple divorces during the term the income interest is payable.

Generation-Skipping Transfer Tax

If an income beneficiary designated by the donor is a "skip person" (i.e., a beneficiary two or more generations removed from the donor) for the purpose of the federal tax on generation-skipping transfers, the creation of that interest may be subject to the skip person tax. In general, skip persons include: (i) grandchildren or more remote descendants of the donor or the donor's spouse; (ii) grandnieces and grandnephews or more remote descendants of the donor's brothers and sisters and the brothers and sisters of the donor's spouse; (iii) grandchildren or more remote descendants of the donor's first cousins and the first cousins of the donor's spouse; and (iv) persons unrelated to the donor who are more than 37.5 years younger than the donor. The donor's spouse is not a skip person, no matter the age difference. If the donor has made a transfer to a skip person, that transfer may be eligible to be sheltered from tax by the allocation to the transfer of a portion of the donor's generation-skipping transfer tax exemption.

Tax on Income Distributed

Income paid out by a Pooled Income Fund is taxable to income beneficiaries. Such income consists of dividend and interest income earned, and in certain circumstances, net short-term capital gains. Income will vary depending upon investment performance and yield. Long-term capital gains, if any, will remain in each Pooled Income Fund, and potentially result in the growth of principal which will ultimately go to the sponsoring charitable organization as the charitable remainder beneficiary.

Securities Laws - Philanthropy Protection Act of 1995

The Philanthropy Protection Act of 1995 (the "Philanthropy Act") amended the federal securities laws to provide nonprofit organizations with additional exclusions and exemptions from registration under the various federal securities laws including the requirements of the Securities Act of 1933, the Securities Exchange Act of 1934, the Investment Company Act of 1940 and the Investment Advisers Act of 1940. The Philanthropy Act amended Section 3(a)(4) of the Securities Act of 1933 (the "Securities Act") to create an exemption from registration under Section 5 of the Securities Act for "any security… of a fund that is excluded from the definition of an investment company under Section 3(c)(10)(B) of the Investment Company Act of 1940 (the "ICA"). Section 3(c)(10)(B) of the ICA provides an exemption for "any security of a fund that is excluded from the definition of an investment company under Section 3(c)(10)(B) of the ICA." That section provides an exemption for any company which is a Pooled Income Fund, or similar fund, maintained by a charitable organization exclusively for the collective investment and reinvestment of assets of a charitable remainder trust, the remainder interests of which are irrevocably dedicated to any charitable organization. The exemption is separate from the not-for-profit exemption in Section 3(a)(4) of the Securities Act, and therefore is not dependent on satisfying the requirements in Release 6175 which the Securities and Exchange Commission had issued in 1980 to provide the outline for no-action against charities that have established Pooled Income Funds without meeting the securities registration requirements.

PIF No Action Letter

The Pooled Income Funds should qualify for the exemption afforded by Section 3(c)(10)(B) of the ICA for Pooled Income Funds since they are maintained by a nonprofit as defined under Code Section 170(b)(1)(A) (other than in clauses (vii) or (viii)), exclusively for the collective investment and reinvestment of assets of one or more funds of one or more charitable organizations. Under Section 3(c)(10)(B) of the ICA, a fund is "maintained" by a charitable organization if the organization serves as a trustee or administrator of the fund or has the power to remove the trustees or administrators of the fund and to designate new trustees or administrators. As such, the sponsoring nonprofit "maintains" the Pooled Income Funds within the meaning of Section 3(c)(10)(B) of the ICA. Also, the nonprofit maintains the Pooled Income Fund exclusively for the investment or reinvestment of assets for the benefit of the sponsor nonprofit and its charitable programs.

While the Philanthropy Act provides exemption from registration for a Pooled Income Fund, the Securities and Exchange Commission still deems the offering of Pooled Income Fund units the sale of a security. As such, the Philanthropy Act does not exempt the fund from the anti-fraud provisions of the securities laws.

Disclosure Statement

Each Pooled Income Fund is required to provide prospective donors with a written statement that provides a full and fair disclosure of the operation of the fund. The statement must be updated annually. This requirement of providing a disclosure statement is not based on any federal tax law requirement, but is an additional requirement under the PIF No Action Letter. In order for a Pooled Income Fund to maintain its exemption from registration under the federal securities rules, the disclosure statement should provide the following information:

i. a description of the sponsoring organization;

ii. a statement regarding the risk to the income distributions and the variable nature thereof;

iii. operation outline of the governing documents for the Pooled Income Fund;

iv. summary of the tax implications to the donor;

v. outline of the operations of the Pooled Income Fund including the investment policy; and

vi. a summary of the process for accepting contributions and the issuance of units.

The gifting disclosure should be updated annually, including financial statements of the Pooled Income Fund.

State Blue Sky Considerations

The Philanthropy Act, in addition to exemption from federal registration requirements under the Investment Company Act of 1940, provided that interests in Pooled Income Funds shall be exempt from any state registration law that requires registration or qualification of securities. However, the Philanthropy Act contained an opt-out provision under which any state could enact a statute providing that the Philanthropy Act does not pre-empt the laws of the state. Several states took advantage of the opt-out provisions.

Any charitable organization that intends to establish a Pooled Income Fund should seek the advice of counsel to determine the applicability of each state's laws.

Continuing Education Questions Suitable for CFP Board

1. What is true about all PIFs?

A. There's an elimination of the capital gains tax on the contributed amount
B. There's a charitable deduction
C. There's an estate tax deduction
D. All of the above

2. What is true about donating property to charities?

A. The large majority are happy to accept property
B. Many have trouble with the liabilities of ownership
C. It must be done directly, since all PIFs are prohibited from accepting real estate
D. Virtually all PIFs accept real estate

3. At the death of the last income beneficiary of a PIF:

A. The remaining principal is transferred to the establishing nonprofit
B. The beneficiary's heir inherits the principal
C. The beneficiary's heir has full discretion on where the money goes
D. The remaining principal goes to up to ten nonprofits named in the will

4. A nonprofit must limit itself to only how many PIFs?

A. One
B. Two
C. There is no limit
D. There is a limit—based on total assets managed

5. What is true about the registration of PIFs?

A. They fall under the Philanthropy Protection Act of 1995
B. They fall under the Investment Company Act of 1940
C. They fall under the Securities Exchange Act of 1934
D. All of the above

6. By law, a PIF is a trust:

A. In which the property transferred by each donor may never be commingled with property transferred by other donors
B. Which cannot have investments in securities which are exempt from taxes
C. For which a donor or beneficiary of an income interest can serve as a trustee
D. All of the above

7. Organizations qualified to establish PIFs include:

A. Churches
B. Publicly supported organizations
C. Hospitals
D. All of the above

8. If a charitable organization maintaining a PIF goes out of existence or loses its qualification,

A. The trustees are likely subject to prosecution
B. The trustees generally have one week to find a new charity
C. The trustees generally have 60 days to find a new charity
D. The fund is dissolved immediately and money returned to donors

9. A PIF must file a *Split-Interest Trust Information Return* (Form 5227) for federal tax purposes.

A. True
B. False

10. Upon contribution, a donor can

A. Retain a income interest
B. Designate an income interest for one living individual—but no more
C. Designate an income interest for two or more living individuals—but no fewer
D. Both A and C

11. The governing declaration of trust must require the distribution of all net income from the PIF to the designated income beneficiaries

A. During the quarter in which the income is earned
B. During the taxable year in which the income is earned
C. During the month in which the income is earned
D. At any time, as long as it's consistent

12. What is true about PIFs' tax filing responsibilities?

A. Form 1041: *U.S. Income tax Return for Estates and Trusts*, must be filed

B. Form 5227: *Split-Interest Trust Information Return*, does not have to be filed

C. Under certain circumstances, Form 4720: *Return of Certain Excise Taxes on Charities*, must be filed

D. Both A and C

13. A PIF pays no capital gains taxes on the sale of appreciated assets that had been held for more than how long?

A. One year

B. One month

C. Seven years

D. Three months

14. If the donor is the sole income beneficiary of the contribution to a PIF, the contribution will not result in any gift tax.

A. True

B. False

15. If the donor names one or more income beneficiaries, other than himself, to receive income from the contribution, the contribution will never be subject to gift tax.

A. True

B. False

16. PIFs were introduced

A. With the Investment Company Act of 1940
B. With the 1969 Tax Reform Act
C. By John Bogle and Vanguard
D. During the Reagan Administration

17. A characteristic of PIFs is that

A. Donors must select and hire trustees
B. Donors must be prepared to handle PIF compliance issues
C. Donors must hire a lawyer to access one
D. They are continuously available to new donors

18. Some grant-making organizations that sponsor PIFs allow donors to recommend other deserving nonprofits to also receive their grants.

A. True
B. False

19. The majority of PIFs are invested in

A. A managed securities portfolio
B. Hedge funds and private equity
C. Mutual funds consisting of debt instruments and equities
D. Both A and C

20. What are generally limitations for PIF donations?

A. Donors must have owned their real estate/securities for longer than one year
B. The minimum acceptable contribution can be as low as $1.5 million for real estate
C. The minimum acceptable contribution an be as low as $500,000 for securities
D. All of the above

21. The solicitation of donations for a PIF is not considered the offering of a security.

A. True
B. False

22. A PIF must have a minimum of how many individual donors?

A. 1
B. 2
C. 7
D. 10

23. Most PIFs are maintained by institutional trustees; the sponsoring organization

A. May maintain the power to remove or replace such organization, or assign it elsewhere
B. Typically assigns choice of trustee to a committee of donors
C. Must maintain the power to remove or replace such organization
D. Is not allowed to change the trustee for a period of two years

24. In calculating the charitable deduction, the valuation of the remainder interest depends on

A. The fair market value of the contribution
B. The age of the named income beneficiaries
C. The rate of return of the PIF
D. All of the above

25. In general, the deduction for an individual donor's aggregate charitable contributions of cash (or of non-appreciated property) within a single tax year is limited to what percentage of the donor's adjusted gross income?

A. 10%
B. 20%
C. 50%
D. 75%

To check your answers, log on at www.fpbooks.com/cecorner.

DISCLAIMER

Please remember that different types of investments involve varying degrees of risk. Therefore, there can be no assurance that the future performance of any type of investment, investment strategy, style, system, or product made reference to directly or indirectly in this booklet will be profitable or equal historical or anticipated performance level(s), or be appropriate for your personal situation. Moreover, you should not assume that any discussion or information contained in this booklet serves as the receipt of, or as a substitute for, personalized investment advice from its authors or from any other investment professional. To the extent that a reader has any questions regarding the applicability/suitability of any specific issue and/or investment discussed in this booklet for his individual situation, he is encouraged to consult with the professional advisor(s) of his choosing.

Glossary

1969 Tax Reform Act: Legislative amendment to the tax code that allowed for the creation of Pooled Income Funds.

1031 Exchange: Section 1031 of the Internal Revenue Code of 1986, as amended, provides for tax deferred exchanges that allow for the sale of an asset and the acquisition of a similar asset without generating a tax liability from the sale of the first asset (also referred to as a "like-kind-exchange"). Real estate is the most heavily used asset in a like-kind-exchange.

401(k): A qualified plan established by employers to which eligible employees may make salary deferral contributions on a post-tax and/or pre-tax basis. Investment earnings on the contributions accrue on a tax-deferred basis.

Annuity: A contract designed to provide payments to the holder at specified intervals and usually after retirement. The holder is only taxed when he or she starts taking distributions or if funds are withdrawn from the annuity account. Annuities are tax deferred; the earnings of the investments are deferred so they cannot be withdrawn without penalty. Annuities are either fixed with guaranteed payment amounts, or variable with payments that will change and typically carry the potential for greater returns. Annuities have death benefit equivalents.

Beneficiary: An individual, institution, trustee or estate which receives or may become eligible to receive certain benefits under a defined contract or by will. Depending on the product, the beneficiary either receives the earnings or income from an investment or the death benefit. For a Pooled Income Fund, there are designated income beneficiaries, as well as the nonprofit sponsor that is the beneficiary of the remaining value upon the death of the last income beneficiary. The distributed value upon death of the last income beneficiary is referred to as the charitable remainder (the equivalent of the death benefit).

Certificate of Deposit: A CD is a short or medium-term, interest-bearing debt investment. Typically offered by banks and FDIC insured, CDs provide higher rates of return than most equivalent duration investments. These rates are provided in exchange for tying up the invested money until maturity of the contract. These are low risk, lower return investments.

Charitable Gift Annuity: An annuity contract established with a public charity. The beneficiaries of the annuity are the donor or the donor's designees, and the holder of the remainder benefit (death benefit) is the charitable organization.

Charitable Remainder Trust: A CRT is a trust established by a donor, to which the donor contributes property and continues to receive income from the property or its re-investment. The donor may designate individual beneficiaries to receive the income and charities to receive the principal after a designated period of time. While contributions to the trust are irrevocable, the donor has control over how the assets of the trust are invested. There are different types of CRTs that provide various income streams. CRTs also provide certain tax benefits to the donors as an irrevocable charitable contribution.

Charitable Tax Deduction: This is the portion of a gift to a qualified charity that is deductible from a donor's federal (and potentially state) income, gift and estate tax calculations.

Code: Internal Revenue Code of 1986 as amended.

CPA: Certified Public Accountant

Declaration of Trust: The document signed by an establishing organization (sponsor) creating a trust into which assets are contributed. A Trustee is appointed to manage the trust, the powers and duties of management of the principal and profit of the trust are stated, and distributions of profits and principal are defined within the declaration of trust.

Disclosure Statement: In compliance with the anti-fraud provisions of securities regulations, a disclosure document (typically referred to as the disclosure statement) provides all of the materially pertinent information associated with a potential investment. This typically includes a discussion of fees, terms, risks, tax implications, investment objectives and other materially relevant facts.

Donor Advised Fund: A private fund created by a nonprofit organization and typically administered by a third party that is established for the purpose of accepting and managing donations on behalf of an organization, family or individual. They offer the donor an easy administration and placement of charitable gifts over time while receiving a charitable tax deduction immediately upon contribution. All income and appreciation from the investments of the fund remain in the fund to be used for additional charitable gifts.

ETF: Exchange traded funds are investment funds that track an index, but can be traded like a stock. ETFs bundle together securities that are in an index and they never track actively managed mutual fund portfolios.

Investment Company Act of 1940: Federal laws which require and regulate the registration and activities of investment companies.

Instrument of Transfer: Legal document outlining the terms of a donor's contribution, including the designation of income beneficiaries and selection of pooled alternatives.

Monte Carlo Simulation: A problem solving technique used to approximate the probability of certain outcomes by running multiple trial runs, called simulations, using random variables. Monte Carlo simulation is named after the city in Monaco, where the primary attractions are casinos that have games of chance that exhibit random behavior.

Net Lease: A lease arrangement that designates the lessee of the property as being solely responsible for all of the costs relating to the asset, in addition to the rent paid under the lease. The structure of this type of lease typically requires the lessee to pay for real estate taxes, insurance requirements and maintenance of the property (also referred to as a triple-net lease).

Nonprofit Organization: An association that is given tax-free status. Donations to nonprofit organizations are typically tax deductible. Examples of nonprofit organizations are charities, hospitals, and schools.

Philanthropy Protection Act of 1995: Congressional legislation that provided amendments to the Investment Company Act of 1940, the Investment Advisers Act of 1940, the Securities Exchange Act of 1934 and the Securities Act of 1933. The overall amendments provided exemptions from registrations for certain charitable related investment products, including Pooled Income Funds.

Additionally, this legislation exempted such charitable investment vehicles from registration under state securities laws unless such states specifically opted out of such exemption.

Pooled Income Fund: A type of mutual fund (exempt from securities registration) comprised of gifts that are pooled and invested together in one account. Income from the fund is distributed to the named beneficiaries according to their share of the fund. A donor to the fund or their named income beneficiaries receive regular distributions of income, and upon death of all of the income beneficiaries, the value of the donor's share of the assets will be distributed to the nonprofit maintaining the fund. A Pooled Income Fund allows a donor to receive perpetual income, claim a current tax deduction and make a future gift to charity.

Public Charity: A nonprofit organization created to support a specific philanthropic cause that qualifies for tax-exempt status under Section 501(c)(3) of the tax code and receives its financial support from a broad base of charitable donations from the general public.

Securities Act of 1933: The first Congressional law regulating the securities industry. It requires registration and disclosure and includes provisions to discourage fraud and deception.

Securities Exchange Act of 1934: This act created the Securities and Exchange Commission, outlawed manipulative and abusive practices in the issuance of securities, required the registration of brokers and listed securities, and required the disclosure of certain financial information and insider trading.

Sponsoring Nonprofit Organization: Nonprofit organization that establishes, maintains and controls a Pooled Income Fund. The sponsoring organization is also the holder of the charitable remainder interests associated with contributions to the Pooled Income Fund.

Tenant-in-Common: Ownership structure for real estate whereby more than one individual shares ownership in a single property. The ownership structure as co-owners provides each owner with an undivided interest in the title to the property. Under Revenue Procedure 2002-22, the Internal Revenue Service provided a series of structural and operational constraints around a tenants-in-common ownership of a property that would allow such an undivided interest to potentially qualify as like-kind property ownership for real estate in a 1031 Exchange.

Units of Participation: Security issued by a Pooled Income Fund that represents the beneficiary's right to the income from the pooled investments. Units are similar to a mutual fund share. However, the unit in a split-interest trust, such as a Pooled Income Fund, represents two ownership interests: (i) that of an income beneficiary; and (ii) the remainder principal value represented by the units, which is the charitable remainder held by the sponsoring nonprofit organization.

www.ingramcontent.com/pod-product-compliance
Ingram Content Group UK Ltd.
Pitfield, Milton Keynes, MK11 3LW, UK
UKHW041444070726
13610UKWH00009B/16